My Book of Poems

Compiled by Ben Cruise
Illustrated by Gloria Solly

A GOLDEN BOOK · NEW YORK
Western Publishing Company, Inc., Racine, Wisconsin 53404

Copyright © 1985 by Western Publishing Company, Inc. Illustrations copyright © 1985 by Gloria Solly. All rights reserved. Printed in the U.S.A. No part of this book may be reproduced or copied in any form without written permission from the publisher. GOLDEN®, GOLDEN & DESIGN®, A GOLDEN BOOK®, and A LITTLE GOLDEN BOOK® are trademarks of Western Publishing Company, Inc. Library of Congress Catalog Card Number: 85-50120 ISBN 0-307-02162-9 / ISBN 0-307-60634-1 (lib. bdg.)
  B C D E F G H I J

Acknowledgments

The editor and publisher have made every effort to trace the ownership of all copyrighted material and to secure permission from copyright holders. Any errors or omissions are inadvertent, and the publisher will be pleased to make the necessary corrections in future printings. Thanks are due to the following authors, publishers, and agents for permission to use the material indicated:

Basil Blackwell Publisher, Oxford, for "Last Song." Doubleday & Company, Inc., for "Barefoot Days" and "I'd Like to Be a Lighthouse," from TAXIS AND TOADSTOOLS, copyright 1926 by Doubleday and Company, Inc., published in the United Kingdom by World's Work as POEMS FOR CHILDREN. Aileen Fisher for "Little Talk," from THAT'S WHY, copyright 1946, renewal 1974; and "Otherwise" from UP THE WINDY HILL, copyright 1953, renewal 1981. Harcourt Brace Jovanovich, Inc., for "Keep a Poem in Your Pocket," from SOMETHING SPECIAL, copyright 1958 by Beatrice Schenk de Regniers. Harper & Row, Publishers, Inc. and Harold Ober Associates Inc., for "Down! Down!" from ELEANOR FARJEON'S POEMS FOR CHILDREN, copyright 1926, 1954 by Eleanor Farjeon. Harper & Row, Publishers, Inc., for "River Winding," from RIVER WINDING, text copyright © 1970 by Charlotte Zolotow, published in the United Kingdom by World's Work. Holt, Rinehart and Winston, Publishers, for "That May Morning," from IS SOMEWHERE ALWAYS FAR AWAY?, copyright 1967 by Leland B. Jacobs. Macmillan Publishing Company and The Society of Authors (on behalf of the copyright owner, Mrs. Iris Wise) for "When You Walk," from COLLECTED POEMS OF JAMES STEPHENS, copyright 1926 by Macmillan Publishing Co., Inc., renewal 1954 by James Stephens. G. P. Putnam's Sons for "The Picnic" and "When," from HOP, SKIP AND JUMP!, copyright 1934, renewal © 1961 by Dorothy Aldis. Rand McNally & Company for "Spring Signs," from *Child Life Magazine,* copyright 1927, 1955 by Rand McNally & Company. Random House, Inc., for "They've All Gone South," from LISTEN—THE BIRDS, copyright 1961 by Pantheon Books, Inc. Viking Penguin, Inc., for "The Hens" and "The People," from UNDER THE TREE, copyright 1922 by B. W. Huebsch, Inc., renewal 1950 by Ivor S. Roberts.

HAPPY THOUGHT

The world is so full of a number of things,
I'm sure we should all be as happy as kings.

Robert Louis Stevenson

OTHERWISE

There must be magic,
Otherwise,
How could day turn to night?
And how could sailboats,
Otherwise,
Go sailing out of sight?
And how could peanuts,
Otherwise,
Be covered up so tight?

Aileen Fisher

RIVER WINDING

Rain falling, what things do you grow?
Snow melting, where do you go?
Wind blowing, what trees do you know?
River winding, where do you flow?

Charlotte Zolotow

WHEN

In February there are days,
Blue, and nearly warm,
When horses switch their tails and ducks
Go quacking through the farm.
When everything turns round to feel
The sun upon its back—
When winter lifts a little bit
And spring peeks through the crack.

Dorothy Aldis

SPRING SIGNS

Everywhere the wind blows
There goes spring—
Red kites and green kites
Are tugging at the string.

Walks have hardly dried
Until marbles roll about
Long before the colored flowers
In the fields are out.

Maybe there is frost yet
And a touch of snow,
But there are little spring signs
Where the children go.

Mildred Bowers Armstrong

CLOUDS

White sheep, white sheep,
On a blue hill,
When the wind stops
You all stand still.
When the wind blows
You walk away slow.
White sheep, white sheep,
Where do you go?

Christina Rossetti

THAT MAY MORNING

That May morning—very early—
As I walked the city street,
Not a single store was open
Any customer to greet.

That May morning—it was early—
As I walked the avenue,
I could stop and stare and window-shop,
And hear the pigeons coo.

Early, early that May morning
I could skip and jump and run
And make shadows on the sidewalk,
Not disturbing anyone.

All the windows, all the lamp posts,
Every leaf on every tree
That was growing through the sidewalk
Seemed to be there just for me.

Leland B. Jacobs

BAREFOOT DAYS

In the morning, very early,
   That's the time I love to go
Barefoot where the fern grows curly
   And grass is cool between each toe,
      On a summer morning—O!
      On a summer morning!

That is when the birds go by
   Up the sunny slopes of air,
And each rose has a butterfly
   Or a golden bee to wear;
And I am glad in every toe—
      Such a summer morning—O!
      Such a summer morning!

Rachel Field

THE PICNIC

We brought a rug for sitting on,
Our lunch was in a box.
The sand was warm. We didn't wear
Hats or shoes or socks.

Waves came curling up the beach.
We waded. It was fun.
Our sandwiches were different kinds.
I dropped my jelly one.

Dorothy Aldis

RAIN

The rain is raining all around,
  It falls on field and tree,
It rains on the umbrellas here,
  And on the ships at sea.

Robert Louis Stevenson

I'D LIKE TO BE A LIGHTHOUSE

I'd like to be a lighthouse
  And scrubbed and painted white.
I'd like to be a lighthouse
  And stay awake all night
To keep my eye on everything
  That sails my patch of sea;
I'd like to be a lighthouse
  With the ships all watching me.

Rachel Field

THE PEOPLE

The ants are walking under the ground,
And the pigeons are flying on the steeple,
And in between are the people.

Elizabeth Madox Roberts

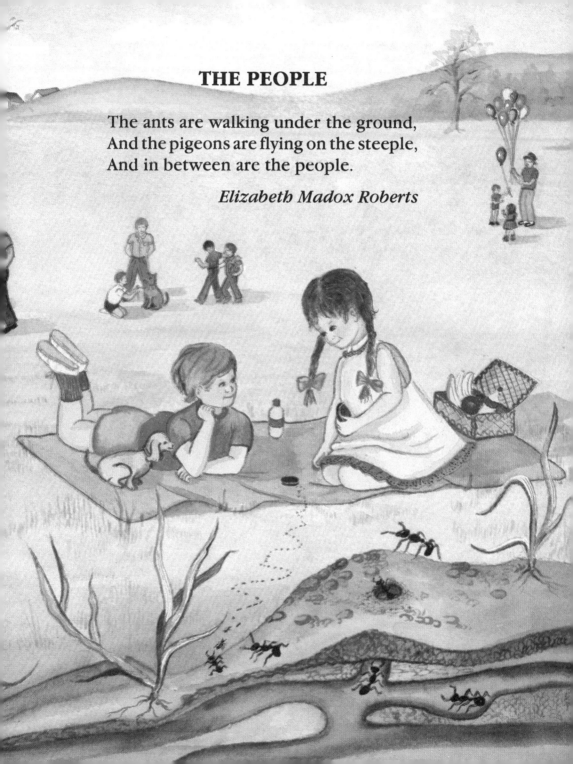

LITTLE TALK

Don't you think it's probable
That beetles, bugs, and bees
Talk about a lot of things—
You know, such things as these:

The kind of weather where they live
In jungles tall with grass
And earthquakes in their villages
Whenever people pass!

Of course, we'll never know if bugs
Talk very much at all,
Because our ears are far too big
For talk that is so small.

Aileen Fisher

WHEN YOU WALK

When you walk in a field,
Look down
Lest you trample
A daisy's crown!

But in a city
Look always high,
And watch
The beautiful clouds go by!

James Stephens

WHO HAS SEEN THE WIND?

Who has seen the wind?
Neither I nor you:
But when the leaves hang trembling,
The wind is passing through.

Who has seen the wind?
Neither you nor I:
But when the trees bow down their heads,
The wind is passing by.

Christina Rossetti

DOWN! DOWN!

Down, down!
  Yellow and brown
The leaves are falling over the town.

Eleanor Farjeon

THEY'VE ALL GONE SOUTH

Redbird, bluebird,
Bird with yellow mouth
All the pretty little birds
Have flown away south,
But the little dusty sparrow
With his wings of rusty brown
For some peculiar reason
Lingers in the town
And little city children
Who wouldn't know a robin
From a cuckoo or a crow
Will hear the little sparrows
Chirping in the snow.

Mary Britton Miller

RING OUT WILD BELLS

Ring out the old,
Ring in the new,
Ring happy bells,
Across the snow!

Alfred, Lord Tennyson

THE HENS

The night was coming very fast;
It reached the gate as I ran past.

The pigeons had gone to the tower of the church
And all the hens were on their perch,

Up in the barn, and I thought I heard
A piece of a little purring word.

I stopped inside, waiting and staying,
To try to hear what the hens were saying.

They were asking something, that was plain,
Asking it over and over again.

One of them moved and turned around,
Her feathers made a ruffled sound,

A ruffled sound, like a bushful of birds,
And she said her little asking words.

She pushed her head close into her wing,
But nothing answered anything.

Elizabeth Madox Roberts

LAST SONG

To the Sun
Who has shone
    All day,
To the Moon
Who has gone
    Away,
To the milk-white,
Silk-white,
Lily-white Star
A fond goodnight
Wherever you are.

James Guthrie

KEEP A POEM IN YOUR POCKET

Keep a poem in your pocket
and a picture in your head
and you'll never feel lonely
at night when you're in bed.

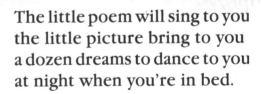

The little poem will sing to you
the little picture bring to you
a dozen dreams to dance to you
at night when you're in bed.

So—
Keep a picture in your pocket
and a poem in your head
and you'll never feel lonely
at night when you're in bed.

Beatrice Schenk de Regniers